Your Tool Kit for Home Selling and Buying

Your Tool Kit for Home Selling and Buying

THE ANSWERS TO ALL THE MYSTERIES

Dave Cochrane

© 2017 Dave Cochrane
All rights reserved.

ISBN: 1973745437
ISBN 13: 9781973745433

*To my wife, Levern—without your love and understanding,
my real-estate career and this book would not be possible.*

Contents

                Preface · ix

Chapter 1 How Is the Market? · · · · · · · · · · · · · · · · · · 1

Chapter 2 What Do I Need to Fix Up? · · · · · · · · · · · · · 5

Chapter 3 How Does the Listing Process Work? · · · · · · 13

Chapter 4 What Do I Do When I Get an Offer? · · · · · · · 21

Chapter 5 What Do I Need to Know When Looking for a House? · 29

Chapter 6 How Do I View a House? · · · · · · · · · · · · · · 33

Chapter 7 What Are the Closing Costs? · · · · · · · · · · · · 37

Chapter 8	Why Should I Hire Dave Cochrane?	41
	Conclusion	45
	Glossary of Terms	47

Preface

I was a broadcaster for twenty-three years. Half of my career was in the Saint John market where I grew up. In 1993, I decided it was time for a change. Radio jobs were shrinking. Collectively my family decided we'd stay in the greater Saint John area of New Brunswick and I would change professions. It wasn't an easy decision. After months of talking to businesspeople, friends and family members, I decided to become a Realtor. It made sense. Radio was a business where you met the public, and so is real estate. That aspect was always enjoyable to me.

I decided to write this book from all the seller and buyer questions and real estate experiences I've enjoyed over the years. I hope it covers all your real-estate questions. I'm here to help.

Chapter 1 of this book is about the local real-estate market and the various types of markets that sellers can sell in and buyers can buy in. Sellers cannot always sell in a seller market, and buyers can't always buy when the market is best for them, usually because of their personal or business situation. Chapter 2 examines all the little and big things you should fix up to get your home looking the best for buyers. You may be thinking of spending more money to fix up your home than you should. Chapter 3 explains all aspects of the listing process, including all the paperwork and various clauses. However, *the most important aspect of this process is to get the list price correct.* Chapter 4 explains what happens when you get an offer. It can be a turbulent time when the seller's hands begin to sweat and the buyer's eyes are as big as hubcaps. Chapter 5 explains all aspects of viewing a home when you're ready to buy. In chapter 6 I talk about what the buyer needs to know and the best system to find a home. It's not a random process. Chapter 7 explains the closing costs for both the buyer and seller. Some closing costs are occasionally overlooked by buyers and sellers. These costs should be calculated before you begin viewing or selling a house. In chapter 8, I answer the question, "Dave, what makes you different from other Realtors?"

This book is a road map to your success in selling or buying a house. Many professionals will come and go throughout the process, but the one professional making sure you don't make any mistakes along the way is me.

CHAPTER 1

How Is the Market?

The number-one question I'm asked as a Realtor is, "How is the market?" The market can be a buyer, seller or balanced market. Picture a clock on the wall. Twelve o'clock is a seller market, and six o'clock is a buyer market. Three o'clock and nine o'clock are balanced markets. The market reflects the economy. A bad economy will reflect a market more suited for a buyer. A good economy reflects a seller market. It's based on the economic theory of supply and demand. If it's a seller market, that means there's less inventory on the market, and the seller has more buyers trying to buy their property. Just the opposite is true if it's a buyer market. There are fewer buyers and more inventory, so a buyer has more homes to choose from. If it's a balanced market, it's just what it says: it's not a buyer or a seller market. It's balanced.

Another question I hear often is, "How long will it take to sell my home?" The answer can vary depending on the type of market. If someone asks me about the greater Saint John market in 2017, it's shifting from a buyer market to a balanced market (right now about 8 o'clock). In a seller market, selling time is less than in a buyer market because there is more demand for houses and less of them. The reverse is true in a buyer market. When a market swings from a seller or buyer market, it first goes through a period as a balanced market. The period of 2006–2008 was the last time we had a seller market in greater Saint John. In 2009, it started to shift to a balanced market. Here's why I believe it happened. Many future sellers decided to put their house on the market during 2006–2008 because of rumours a second oil refinery was to be built in east Saint John. They wanted to capitalize on what they perceived to be a seller's market coming up. Buyers, also aware of the upcoming refinery, bought, sellers sold and then the refinery project was cancelled in 2009. There would be a lot of people in the east side selling to move elsewhere after the cancellation announcement. There now was less demand and more inventory, a buyer market.

I'm also frequently asked, "How do I find houses I want to view in the market?" No problem. I can enter you in my *Buyer Search System*, which will send you new listings in your requested area and price range. These listings come from all real-estate companies, and you can get them though my system quicker and in more detail than you can on public sites. I have found that half the sellers want to find their new home before they list theirs and the other half want to put theirs on the market and then look for a new home. Either way I can help you.

YOUR TOOL KIT FOR HOME SELLING AND BUYING

If you are going to put your house up for sale, you'll want to have an idea of the average percentage of the list price the house will sell for and how long it will take to sell. In this market heading from a buyer market to a balanced market, it is about 95 percent of the list price. It takes about 120 days to sell a house. For my listings, I'm selling for a higher percentage in less than market average time.

The Saint John Real Estate Board can also provide past years history of the market.

CHAPTER 2

What Do I Need to Fix Up?

When I visit your home for the first time, you and I walk through it, talking about the pros and cons of your home and things that should be fixed up before putting it on the market.

Many sellers think they know everything that needs to be fixed up, but that's not always true.

I had a house on the west side for sale. One day I called to talk to the husband about something he had asked me. His wife said he was on his way to an electrical store to buy a breaker panel to replace his fuse panel. A man had driven by the house and saw the For Sale sign out front. He had come to the door and asked to see the house, and the seller had let him in. (That's a no-no for two reasons: the security of your home, and if he's serious about buying the house, he'll call my number on the For Sale sign, call his Realtor if he has one and we'll set up an appointment.) The seller let him look around, and when he saw the fuse panel, he said that the house wouldn't sell with a fuse panel. The seller needed a breaker panel. He said it was easier to sell the house with breakers. I contacted the seller on his mobile phone and talked him out of buying the new panel. It would have cost him around $2,000. This was about fifteen years ago. Back then, fuse panels were not as much an issue as they are today. By the way, the house sold with no mention from the buyer about the fuse panel. This story is a classic example of why it's always a good idea to have me visit the home *first* before you start fix-ups. My goal is for you to get the house looking it's best while spending the least amount of money.

One of the biggest seller problems I notice is woodstoves. They're not as popular as they were, and some can be old and not up to the woodstove standards of the day. In many houses with older woodstoves, the insurance company will "grandfather" the woodstove, giving insurance to the owner even if it's a little old. However, if you have an older woodstove that doesn't meet the current woodstove requirements and you sell your home, all bets are off. Another insurance company working with the buyer will probably not insure the house unless that woodstove is up to code or removed from the house. My suggestion would be to call a woodstove company. Have them come out, even if it costs a few dollars, to inspect the woodstove and make sure it meets all the codes before putting the house on the market. When you have an accepted offer and everybody's excited you don't need a building inspector saying the woodstove doesn't meet code. On closing, any appliances you are leaving need to be in working order. Heating appliances like a furnace or propane stove that need fuel, should also be in working order for the building inspection.

YOUR TOOL KIT FOR HOME SELLING AND BUYING

The inspector will be checking them if they are to remain as part of the agreement. Heat pumps are becoming popular but the most popular heating system for clients I've worked with during my career is baseboard hot water. They like the fact the pipe will still be hot and give off extra heat even after the furnace stops at the set temperature.

Another good question to ask if you're selling your home: "Is my chimney in working order?" If there's a fireplace in the house and it's not working, it could be expensive to put in a liner. I'd suggest getting a couple of estimates and see if you can get the chimney fixed. Why? Because the buyer is thinking, "If that fireplace is not in working order, what else in the house is there that I can't see that may not be up to standards?" It puts apprehension in the mind of the buyer, and that's the last thing you want. Most homeowners I've met have never been in their attic. It's a good idea to push up the hatch, turn on a flashlight, and view the inside and insulation. Look for dampness inside the roofing, and make sure the insulation is spread properly throughout. A building inspector will be looking up there, so you don't want any surprises. Make sure there are no screws securing the attic hatch(s) or other doors the inspector will want to open. Building inspectors will not unscrew anything. They need easy access around the home and property. They will check wall outlets, power panels etc. If they can't get at something to view it closely they won't move objects. They don't want the liability if something breaks.

What about hardwood floors and stairs? Are they in good shape? If they're badly scratched, they should be refinished.

It wouldn't be expensive because you'll get a partial return on your money when your home sells. In many home designs the first thing a buyer will notice when they walk in the front door is the stairs. Hardwood floors and stairs are considered an upgrade to a buyer. They'll pay a bit more for them. If they're severely scratched its a minus for the buyer. My opinion is you will net more money by refinishing them and then selling the house for a bit more money. Buyers don't want to buy a house and then do major work. They want it done before they buy and will pay extra for it. Strip off any wallpaper and paint the wall a neutral colour. You could put up new wallpaper you love, have your friend over for coffee and they hate it. It's a very personal taste and not as acceptable to a buyer as a neutral painted wall.

Painting is the number one thing you can do to get the most return on your money. Take a can of paint, maybe some crack fill, and go through the house. Touch up all the scratches, dents, and nicks. You can use an old facecloth to dab in the paint bucket and then touch up spots. It leaves the same texture as the paint on the wall, with no brush strokes.

One of the most popular buyer questions I'm asked is, "How old is the roof?" What they usually mean is, "How old are the roof shingles?" A roof is a major expense. A buyer doesn't want to buy a house, and then spend thousands immediately on new roof shingles and/or the roof wood under the shingles. A roof is something you can't ignore if there is a problem. If your roof has a few missing shingles, you should get a roofer and have them repaired. A while

YOUR TOOL KIT FOR HOME SELLING AND BUYING

ago I visited a seller who had recently put on new shingles because the old shingles had leaked continuously. I looked at the ceilings and saw some wet marks. The seller said they were from the old roofing and were not new leaks. I explained that the buyer will see those leaks and may not even mention it to their Realtor so that the Realtor can ask me about the marks. They may think it's a leaky roof and go to the next house. I explained that scenario to the seller, he fixed the old ceiling stains and the house eventually sold.

Windows are another important consideration. Clean all the windows inside and out. When the windows are opened, make sure you don't forget to clean out the dirt in and around the windowsills. Caulk around the outside of the windows if required. Vinyl windows are better than wood windows. They're more energy efficient, will get you more money when selling your home and last longer.

Make sure, if you have a furnace, you know its age and have all the paperwork to prove that it has been maintained. Same with an oil tank.

Is the electrical entrance fuses or breakers? An electrician could look at your fuse panel and say that it's fine—but that's an electrician. The insurance company or the buyer would much rather have breakers. When you're selling you'll have to reflect it in the price if you don't want to replace the fuse panel with a breaker panel. Back in the day knob and tube wiring was the accepted norm before fuse panels. I've had cases where the seller had disconnected knob and tube and installed a breaker panel. The insurance company, however, would not insure the house till the knob and tube was not only disconnected but also removed from the house. Make sure the interior of the home is updated as much as possible, including new light fixtures if the current ones are hopelessly outdated. Also make sure all the light bulbs are in working order. You may think it's a small thing, but if there are burned-out bulbs, the buyer is thinking that phrase I keep mentioning: "what else is the seller not taking care of that I can't see?" Update the door, kitchen cupboard knobs and handles if they're outdated. Touch up the cupboard doors if water has stained them in places over the years. Clean out the dryer vent. If there is a new kitchen, the house is obviously worth more than one that has a thirty-year-old kitchen. The same with the bathrooms; if the bathrooms are outdated, then that must be reflected in the price. Scrape off the old caulking around the tub, and redo it with a nice fresh coat. Mildew on tubs is a major turnoff for buyers. They will pull back the bath curtain or shower door to check. Do your door bells work? Oil squeaky doors and hinges. Speaking of squeaky, make sure squeaks are removed in floors; you may need to hire a carpenter but if they're fixed it won't be a turn off for buyers. I once had a buyer ask me if the floor was falling in because it squeaked.

Clean the rain gutters and check the weather stripping. Replace worn deck boards and stain the deck(s) if they need it if you've had a few weeks of dry weather so the stain can adhere to dry wood. Many homes over twenty-five years old have bumpy ceilings, some long or some shorter (called popcorn or spackle finish). It was the ceiling style of the day. The younger the buyer the less they like it. If you decide to tackle the issue, you can scrape the ceiling, crack fill any dents, clean it, paint it, or you can knock off the high points and put a new ceiling over the bumps, which would only drop the ceiling marginally. Either option would brighten and update the house. Most people have a hot water tank. Check the date on the tank. If it's over 12 years old call your energy provider and ask if it should be replaced. The interior fiberglass liner will eventually rust and you'll have forty gallons of water on your basement floor. If need be, they'll install a new one and take away the old tank. Most homeowners rent their tanks from their energy provider so there would be no charge for this procedure. If you know it's a stainless-steel liner they are good for over twenty years. Fix leaky faucets, running toilets and tighten all your closet door knobs. Tidy up your closets to make them appear as big as possible and if they have a fabric covering instead of a door get a door installed. If you're thinking of ripping up some carpet don't put new carpet back down if you can help it. Buyers tell me they like laminate, ceramic or hardwood. There's no dust, easier to clean and not as many allergies circulating through the house. I believe that's what started the hardwood craze years ago. Many houses built in the fifties and sixties in this area were constructed with hardwood floors main level. Then they installed carpet over the hardwood. In the new millennium that's a strange thing to do but back then homeowners liked the warmer carpet. About twenty years ago people started ripping up the carpet and finishing the hardwood underneath. New houses generally have hardwood floors installed. I've had many mothers tell me hardwood is better than carpet to relieve their children's allergies. In the yard keep the lawn mown and tree branches trimmed. Make sure, if you have pets, you do regular maintenance on what they leave behind on the lawn. Take away items in the yard you don't need or store them out of sight. Regularly pull weeds in the flower beds. Tidy up the shed and garage, if you have them, to make them look bigger and easier for the buyer to walk around in. I've had more than one husband say they loved the garage and after finding out their wife loved the interior of the home they bought it. He didn't care about the house if he got his garage. You may want to pressure wash the house. It may look clean but you'd be surprised how much brighter it will look after the wash. A well cared for exterior of the house and yard makes a difference to a buyer. It's called *curb appeal* and puts the buyer in a positive frame of mind about your home even before they view the inside. It's no mistake that sellers who use the suggestions in this book sell their homes before others.

Make sure you have a visible house number out front! This may seem elementary, but I can't tell you how many times, especially at night, the buyer and I have been unable to see a number. Not all sellers have a For Sale sign out front. (don't ask me why). Emergency responders will thank you too.

CHAPTER 3

How Does the Listing Process Work?

The selling system starts with me talking to you on the phone to get some answers to questions about your house. This helps give me a better idea of what I'll see before I visit you. It also helps me with my homework on the house's value. When I arrive, with all homeowners there, you show me through your home, and we talk a little bit more about the house as we view it.

After we go through your home, we come back to the kitchen table. There are four pieces of paper to sign. One is a four-page document called the property condition disclosure statement(PCDS). It's a seller questionnaire about the history of your property to the best of your knowledge. This document answers a lot of buyer questions. If they want to read it after a showing that's good news for you. It shows further interest. Make sure you don't forget anything. Disclose everything about the house to the best of your knowledge, or it could come back to haunt you at the buyer's building inspection. I've had buyers upset because the seller got some answers wrong on the PCDS and the buyer thought the seller should have known the correct answers. The buyer lost trust in the seller and walked from the deal. Disclosing everything and forgetting nothing means that the buyer will base their offer on the PCDS and other factors. They won't try for a lower price after the inspection because of a problem the inspector found that wasn't disclosed in the PCDS. That's because they already know all the history of the house before the inspection, not just some. You can hire a building inspector to inspect your home *before* you list it to make sure you know all the issues, if any, with your home. It also will save you a lot of anxiety at the buyer's inspection.

The other three papers include the data sheet, which has the measurements, pictures and other pertinent information about the house. It is what a buyer sees when they get a listing emailed from their Realtor. There are two schools of thought regarding appliances. Washer, dryer, fridge, stove can cost $3000 in 2017. That's a big expenditure for a buyer. You can include them on the data sheet as remaining or leave them out. When you leave them out of the listing (but you really don't want to move them after closing) a buyer may ask for them anyway. To the buyer it looks like they're getting more for their money if you leave the appliances. The dishwasher is usually a built-in so it remains, being an attachment to the property. The other option is to include them in the listing to make it more attractive for the buyer. Most sellers include them in the listing. They feel if they don't, they have less chance to sell than other sellers who leave them as an

YOUR TOOL KIT FOR HOME SELLING AND BUYING

extra. There is also an agency form and a listing agreement to fill out. The agency form explains that I am working for you the seller. My job is to get the home sold for the highest possible amount of money in the shortest amount of time with the least hassle. Buyer Realtors work for the buyer. Their job is to get the most house for the least amount of money.

Whichever party the Realtor is working for is explained in writing to the client. Any conversations they have not relating to the listing are confidential and cannot be discussed with anyone. It's called a "fiduciary" relationship, which means a high level of trust. It's the same relationship you would have with a lawyer who represents you. One other paper that doesn't need your signature but needs to be filled out is the FINTRAC form. Real estate is a business where cash can be used for a transaction. Criminals have laundered their money through real estate for years. This federal paper requires you to produce a photo I.D, like a driver's licence, so I can take down the information. Everyone who buys or sells real estate in Canada must fill out this form.

I also show you my *Comparative Market Analysis* (CMA). I talk about houses like yours that have sold in the area in the last few years. If you go further back than that in the greater Saint John area, the market prices would not reflect current market value. I also check your current competition on the market as well as expired listings, houses that were listed but did not sell. They usually expire because the price of the house was too high. It's bad news for the seller because when buyers see a house on the market for a long time they think there must be something wrong with it. When I became a Realtor, trainers would tell me buyers think there is something wrong with the house if it sits on the market too long and doesn't sell. I didn't believe it at the time but in my experiences over the years I've learned it's true. The language I use when talking to you about suggestions for your home is the buyer talking, not my own. It's what a buyer will be thinking when going through your home. All these factors are collectively called *fair market value*. To begin calculating it, after asking many questions to you on the phone before our appointment, I'll check the size and condition of the house, the age, and many other considerations. Age is a big deal. A house on its own land built in 1960 was built for a lot less than a house built in 1980. The construction materials and price of the lot would make, all other things with the two houses being equal, the 1980 home worth more money.

Another factor that makes a big difference in the price is a garage. There could be a $10,000–$15,000 difference in price depending on whether there is one and how old or big it is. I'll also look at the assessed tax value determined by the New Brunswick Assessment Department. I will discuss it with you because that's usually the only value you know about your home. I don't put a lot of stock in it. Realtors deal with fair market value to determine a list price range for the house, not assessed value. The number of bedrooms helps determine value. Four bedrooms upstairs is better for a buyer looking for a four-bedroom house than three up and one in the basement. When I'm talking to the seller on the

YOUR TOOL KIT FOR HOME SELLING AND BUYING

phone before I visit their home the seller may say they have two bedrooms main level and a den. No, if it has a closet and an *egress* window the seller has three bedrooms main level. *Egress* means the window must be a certain size to get out of in case of fire. The more bedrooms you have the better. The final paper on the table is the listing agreement and includes the commission and the period the house is listed (among other details.) The commission is usually split in half between the listing company and the buying company. The real-estate companies get their share of the commission on closing and then give their Realtor whatever share they agreed to in the Realtor's company agreement. All documents to sign are explained in detail line by line. It's a good idea to have a For Sale sign. On average, around 10 percent of a Realtor's business comes from buyer sign calls because they saw the sign out front. Buyers like to drive around after they've made the decision to buy a house. A For Sale sign may be the first time they see your home for sale. At that point, they'll call the listing Realtor or a Realtor they are working with and make an appointment to view your home. I explain all the marketing. Every Realtor's marketing strategy is different. I will also have buyers looking for houses in a certain area and price range, so I'll be thinking whether I have a buyer who may want to see your home.

There are several ways to highlight your home's value in the marketing strategy. If the home has southern exposure, make sure that is written in the house listing description. This means the sun is visible most of the day and evening on a certain part of the property. That's a plus for the buyer.

DAVE COCHRANE

I probably sound like Scrooge, but I advise taking down all the family pictures when the house is on the market. When buyers are viewing a home, they want to picture themselves living in it. They can't do that when family pictures remind them it's someone else's home. When you're selling in the winter, much of the property could be covered in snow, making it hard for the buyer to know what is underneath. Put three or four summertime exterior colour pictures on the kitchen table for buyers to see when coming through your home. They'll appreciate it. In winter keep the driveway and walkways clear of ice and snow including the deck. I had a winter listing where the seller didn't keep the driveway clear. More than one buyer's car slid down the sloped driveway. What do you think the odds they bought it? Make sure you paint any rooms a neutral colour like beige or linen. With a neutral palette, buyers can better picture their own décor choices.

I take pictures and put them to music. I also give a written explanation on each picture what the buyer is viewing. It can help give the buyer a better idea of the layout of the home. Not many Realtors in my market do this type of video marketing. It is called a *virtual tour*.

The house then goes up for sale, usually through MLS. The Multiple Listing Service, is the foundation of a Realtor's business. In the greater Saint John area, there are hundreds of Realtors associated with MLS from all companies. Realtors can show other companies' listings by going through the listing Realtor to book appointments. It's unusual in business for a company to work with a competitor, but that's what Realtors do. When I offer the home for sale I am the only Realtor in contact with you. I take care of everything.

CHAPTER 4

What Do I Do When I Get an Offer?

When I receive an offer from the buyer Realtor, I call you, and we discuss the offer. Then we decide what we want to do with it. Sometimes a seller will counter and that's their bottom line. Some buyers won't pay more than their initial offer. Generally, there's going to be another counteroffer back from the buyer after you counter the buyer's initial offer. That may not happen, but in this market, that's usually the case. This may go back and forth a few times until the two sides agree to terms in the offer. Money is not the only important factor, so is the closing date. When going through the offer I always suggest you do not agree to do any work on the property that the buyer wants done at your expense and OK'd by the buyer before closing. I suggest you both agree to a new lower sale price in writing based on the buyer expert's written estimate of price and work to be done. Then the buyer will take care of the issue after closing. If you can't avoid it get a written estimate yourself of work to be done so you have proof of the cost and description. You don't need a buyer coming back to inspect work to be done by you and it's not what they expected. That can hold up closing. A written estimate is a good idea for two reasons. You'll know the cost if you must do the work or the buyer has the estimate in writing to get the work done after closing. The attachments to the property, that remain and are mentioned in the offer, include bath fixtures, light fixtures, carpet, cushion floor, drapery tracks and curtain rods. However, window coverings such as drapes, blinds etc. are not attached. They must be specifically written in the offer if you want them to remain. Whether you're the buyer or seller, bite your lip if you get upset with the other party during negotiations. If someone seems to be upset, the other side could dig in—and no one wins in that scenario. Once the offer is accepted, included in the offer are *conditions*. At this point we're only half way to getting everything done. The most important condition for the buyer to remove is a finance approval letter from the buyer's financial institution (a bank or mortgage company) stating that they have the money to buy the house. Although buyers are preapproved before they start looking at houses, financial institutions go into greater detail of buyers' finances before sending an approval letter to the buyer's Realtor as part of the written agreement. From there, it is forwarded to me as the listing Realtor and I'll notify you. One condition the financial institution may have is for an *appraiser*, hired by the financial institution, to view the home to verify that it is worth as much or more money than the buyer was loaned. A qualified appraiser should be licensed or certified and be familiar with the local area. They must be impartial and have

YOUR TOOL KIT FOR HOME SELLING AND BUYING

no direct or indirect interest in the transaction. They'll do a written report, which takes a day or two, and send it to the financial institution. If everything is OK, the financial institution issues the finance approval letter to the buyer Realtor who forwards it to me as the listing Realtor. If the house appraisal is less than the agreed price, the deal could fall apart, or the buyer can try to find some money to give to the deal which would be the difference between the appraised value and the higher selling price.

Buyers usually will get a professional building inspector to view the property, but not all the time. Sometimes a friend or family member will do the inspection. I suggest hiring a professional. It takes three to four hours and costs around $500. Or, you can hire an electrician, plumber, contractor and other professionals to inspect various aspects of your home. Each of these professionals would probably charge you an hour's work, but make sure you check. I had a father confident in his ability to do an inspection for his daughter despite my objection. His inspection was forty-five minutes. She bought the house and the next spring the basement flooded. At the end of the inspection the buyers and their Realtor will usually arrive at the property to discuss the inspection with the inspector. Three things can happen. Either the buyers have no problems with the inspection, they have some issues to discuss with you through the Realtors, or there are too many issues, and they walk away from the deal. That's their prerogative. The buyers must be happy with removing all their conditions, or they have the right to walk away from the deal. In my experience, very seldom does that happen. After all, both you and the buyer are motivated to get the house sold.

The buyers also need a letter from their insurance company that says they can get insurance on the property when the deal closes. Years ago, the New Brunswick Real Estate Association's Forms Committee added an insurance clause in the purchase and sale agreement. Why? Because some buyers were waiting until just before closing to get insurance. That could be a problem because an insurance company may have issues with the property. In that case, they wouldn't give insurance until they were resolved. The bigger problem was the closing could be held up until the issues were deemed acceptable, which would inconvenience a lot of people.

There will be a water test if the home is on a well, and it is paid for by the buyer. Financial institutions will not give buyers a mortgage if the well water is bad. Even if you weren't getting a mortgage, you wouldn't want bad water at closing. In 2017, it was around $55 for a basic test. In New Brunswick, for the basic test, there can be no bacteria in the water. If it is present, you must clean the water (shock the well) at your own expense and then re-test for acceptance. Shocking the well requires you to put bleach down the well, which kills the bacteria, run it through all the house water lines, wait a day and then flush out the bleach. Then the water is re-tested. I would recommend asking the water test company who took the initial test to shock the well. You don't need the hassle and it's well worth the money. Then the water is re-tested. *You or*

YOUR TOOL KIT FOR HOME SELLING AND BUYING

the buyer should never take a water sample. Who's to say you didn't get the sample from some other house to make sure it passed or the buyer tainted it to make sure it failed so they could get out of the deal. Have your water-test company, an independent third party, take the sample to avoid any liability.

If the water is still bad after the re-test you must pursue other measures to clear the bacteria. Your water test company can help. Even if the buyer walks from the deal at this point you still need to cure the issue. Your home is still on the market and the well needs to be fixed for the next buyer. Because the issue is part of the history of the property you must disclose to future buyers there was a problem but you corrected it. There can also be an extended test if the buyer puts it in the offer. It tests the top twenty-five mineral levels in the water as well as doing the basic test. It costs around $250 in 2017 and the levels must be within provincial guidelines to pass. Buyers are ok with seller problems if the seller has corrected them. If a seller discloses in the PCDS they had a little water cleaned up with a mop during a wind storm and the buyer bought the house the buyer is ok with it. However, if the seller didn't disclose the water issue and the buyer discovered it after closing during a heavy rain they're upset. Same water, same issue but one seller disclosed it and one did not.

At this point, if all other conditions are met, the buyer provides a money deposit to hold the house until closing. It is their money, but it will be forfeited to you and the listing company if the buyers do not buy the house under the terms of the purchase and sale agreement. This rarely happens.

The offer could contain other conditions, but these are the main ones. The buyer removal of conditions usually takes a week to ten days, depending on the time limit in the offer. Then the Sold sign goes up. Some buyers, at this point, will call the seller directly and ask if they can store some items in the seller's house till closing. *Do not agree to this request.* You do not need the liability. Buyer items stored in your home are not insured. They call you directly because they know there is no way the Realtors or lawyers would agree to the request. I'm often asked when you and the buyer need a lawyer. After all conditions are met in an accepted offer, your real-estate company sends all the documents to your and the buyer lawyer so they can get the paperwork ready to transfer the house to the new owners on closing.

The last thing for buyers to do is a final walk-through the day before or the day of closing. At that time, the house must be in the condition that the buyer agreed to in the accepted offer. Then, after the final walk-through, the buyers call their lawyer and give him or her the OK, and the house closes, usually around noon the day of closing. Keys can be left with the lawyer but make sure one key is given to the buyer Realtor to hold for the buyer till closing. It could be inconvenient for the buyer to get the keys right away from their lawyer after closing. It's nice to have a key to get in their

YOUR TOOL KIT FOR HOME SELLING AND BUYING

new home as soon as it closes. Closing is the time and date at which the buyers now own the home and you must be completely gone. Everything that will not remain, according to the accepted offer, must be off the property. Then the buyers excitedly head for the home with the keys, and you head to the bank with the sale money.

CHAPTER 5

What Do I Need to Know When Looking for a House?

When you're the seller and have an accepted offer on your home, you will now be wearing a different hat as a buyer. I have a ton of information I can give you whether you are a first-time buyer or experienced. We can go over closing costs, a written promise as to what I'll do as your buyer Realtor, a moving check-list of who to notify before you move, an agency explanation, the PCDS explanation and a CMHC brochure. Canada Mortgage and Housing Corporation are a federal agency who insure your loan if your down payment is less than twenty percent. There's more about CMHC in the glossary. The first thing I need to know as your buyer Realtor is your price range, specifics you want in a house and in what area(s) you want to buy a home. Then I can enter you in my *Buyer Search System*, which will e-mail you every active listing from every real-estate company in that price range and area. Then every day after that, the new ones will drip to you. You'll get them quicker than by looking on a public site because you won't have to search the entire market looking for homes in your preferred area and price range. They're also more detailed coming from me. I work with an intranet program of MLS not the public property sites.

The next step is to contact me with houses you want to view. I contact the listing Realtors to set up a time and day to view them. Buyers, please be on time for showings. You're Realtor is probably busy and being late throws their entire schedule off including being late for your other showings. If you're bringing small children please keep them with you in the home. We all love children but don't let them run around unsupervised, play with children's toys or touch anything. You'd think everyone knows these courtesies. No! I've had a few ticked off sellers call me after a showing saying toys were everywhere. One time I was showing a house to a buyer. He came around a corner and knocked a metal plate off a stand. On its way to the floor it chipped a valuable coffee table. The buyer paid for the table to be repaired but always watch where you're going. You never know what you may run in to. I've also had instances where a seller did not want to sell. It was a breakup. Only one of two owners lived in the house and even though the seller wanted to stay they couldn't afford it without the other owner's income, who had moved out. Therefore, it went on the market. Unfortunately, even though the spiteful owner must sell they didn't make it easy for buyers to see the house. "The time is not convenient" they said. "It's too short notice to get the house ready to show" they said. I know a seller who had their dog pee on the living room carpet to dissuade any buyers from buying

YOUR TOOL KIT FOR HOME SELLING AND BUYING

the house. Once you get in the house it's messy with dishes in the sink, beds not made, clothes everywhere. In this case you must overlook the seller roadblocks. Some buyers can, some can't. Patience is a virtue. Some houses have tenants who give the Realtors grief by forgetting about an appointment. They can't be told to leave for a showing but they will be asked by the seller when booking the showing. I had one tenant stay and tell my buyer the roof leaked and the owner wasn't doing anything about it. The roof didn't leak. The tenant figured if he cast the house in a bad light no one would buy it and he wouldn't have to move. It takes longer to sell these types of properties. Most buyers travel house to house in their vehicle instead of with me. I feel they need some private time to talk about the houses they've seen. The exception is when I'm working with out-of-town clients. They don't know the market so it's best they stay with me so we don't lose each other in traffic. The seller will not be home when we go to see the house, because we want you to feel as comfortable as possible when viewing the home. You can't do that if you are opening doors and cupboards with the seller sitting there. Buyers think they're buying with their head. Most times they buy with their heart. I had a buyer tell me he absolutely, positively, whole heartedly had to have a six-and-a-half foot living room wall for his extra-long leather sofa. He'd bring a measuring tape with him to measure the wall in different condos. Finally, we found the home they loved and they bought it. When they were moving in they discovered the sofa was too long to get turned in the hall to go straight in the door to the living room. They sold the sofa because they couldn't get it in the door. Once you find your dream home, we'll write an offer. You may be in competition with another buyer or buyers who are fighting for that house. It's called a multiple offer situation. The seller can accept the best offer after informing all potential purchasers that other offers are on the table and inviting them to make their best offer; the seller can counter one offer while putting the other offers to the side awaiting a decision on the counteroffer; or the seller can counter one offer and reject the others. It sounds like crazy stuff, but I'll see you through it.

When you're not in a multiple-offer situation, we write an offer, and I present it to the seller's Realtor. Then the seller either accepts the offer, counters it back or they reject it entirely. Most of the time there's a counter. If the seller counters the offer and you can't live with that either you have three choices. You may counter again, say that your previous counter was your best offer, or walk away. Hopefully the two sides finally come to an agreement and there is an accepted offer. Next, we go through the conditions process for about a week to ten days, depending what the purchase and sale agreement states, just like you did when you were selling your home.

CHAPTER 6

How Do I View a House?

As a seller, you must prepare your home for viewing. It needs to be bright, open, and spacious. You're not going for a homey look—you're going for a pristine atmosphere. In the pictures I'll take, we don't want the dog sleeping on the floor with the newspaper on the footstool and people lounging by the fireplace. We're showing off the home, not people or pets. Make sure you don't have too much furniture in rooms. It makes the rooms look smaller. Small, closed in and dark is bad. Spacious, open and bright is good. I showed a house to a buyer and the seller had staged the house themselves. They had lovely furniture in the rooms but there was so much you could hardly turn around. The seller thought the furniture was the star. That's true to a point but, at the end of the day, the house is the star. Put price tags on anything you want to sell around the house. Some people think that's tacky but many buyers appreciate it and will buy seller items. That's good news for you. Less to move and some extra quick money. When setting up the process for showing your home, we decide how the buyers are going to get in. Along with the day, they'll give an hour window. The Realtor gives that time frame because they could be showing other houses. A buyer could be in one home for five minutes and another a lot longer. The buyer's Realtor either leaves it unlocked, locks it after the showing, or as the selling Realtor I can put on a lockbox. Modern lockboxes can only be accessed by a Realtor. Each Realtor has a code on his or her phone, gets the key for entry from inside the lockbox, and then puts it back in the lockbox after showing. Make sure that besides the house key you also give me keys for any out-buildings such as a shed or detached garage. Those keys are sometimes forgotten. When houses are built the design is for a wow factor when you enter the home through the front door. That will not happen if the buyer must come in a garage or kitchen door. Buyers may need to come and view a home at various times that may not be convenient for you. When you make the home easier to show, it's usually easier to sell. For showings leave your house and take everyone, including the pets. Make sure Fluffy's litter box is clean and pet food dishes and beds are put away. I had a closing where the only thing left in the house when we went for the final walk through was a full litter box in the basement. The buyer and I opened the front door and almost fell over from the smell. We think the seller was upset about the sale price and was getting back at the buyer. You never know. Buyers don't come back very often if they can't see the house when they want. A few

YOUR TOOL KIT FOR HOME SELLING AND BUYING

years ago, one of my sellers decided to take his house off the market for a month despite my objection. He was having guests from out of town coming to stay and didn't want constant interruption trying to get the house ready to show. During the time it was off the market, I had ten Realtors wanting to show it, but the seller refused all. I took the Realtors' names and called them back when we put it back on the market. *Not one buyer was still looking for a house.* They had all bought another one.

While showing buyers one of my homes at an open house, there was a meowing cat outside the kitchen door trying to get in. I opened the door, he came in and went to the cat dish. Later, after open house ended, and I locked up and left. Later in the day, I called the seller to let her know about the success of the open house. During the conversation she said, "Dave, who owns the cat on my bed?" Much to my embarrassment the cat on her bed was not hers but belonged to a neighbour down the street. The seller had a cat but had taken it with her because of the open house. I didn't know she took the cat. She was a good sport about it and we had a laugh, but it taught me a valuable lesson: if an animal is in, don't let it out, and if an animal is out, don't let it in. Also, here's a golden rule at showings: always look to the floor when opening a door. You never know what may be behind it.

CHAPTER 7

What Are the Closing Costs?

Whether buying a house or having just sold one, there are costs at closing for both the buyer and seller.

First the seller. As the seller, your lawyer will calculate how many days of the year before closing you've owned the home because you only pay taxes (property, water/sewerage among others depending on the home) on the number of days that year you owned the house. If you're on a well, there would be no water tax, just sewerage. The lawyers will also calculate other expenses owed on closing. One of the last things you should do is to make sure you repair any scratches or dents caused by moving out. Some sellers will also hire a cleaning company to clean up after they've moved instead of doing it themselves. It's busy for everyone and can save a lot of seller's time. You don't need complaints about an unkempt house at final walk-through. You and the buyer usually meet with your lawyer a few days before closing to sign all the paperwork. You should check with a few lawyers to find out their fees, which can vary.

There are more expenses for the buyer than the seller. First, during the conditions process, as the buyer you gave a deposit to hold the house till closing. Your lawyer knows that and will talk to you about it when you meet. The provincial government charges a "transfer tax" to you on closing; it's 1 percent of the purchase price. You should calculate, as the seller did, the number of days that year you will own the house, and you'll pay the appropriate sewerage and/or water and property taxes on that figure at closing. There may be other taxes but these are the most common. Every deal is different.

Title insurance is good to have and costs around $250. It protects you on a variety of issues after closing; your lawyer will explain it to you. If there are fuel tanks on the property, the seller will fill them as part of the agreement, and you will pay for a full fuel tank(s) on closing. We may be able to negotiate savings on the fuel when writing the offer by adding "no fuel adjustment on closing." That means the seller will not top off the fuel tank(s) on closing, and whatever fuel is in the tank(s) belongs to you at no expense. You will have to pay for all service hookups, and don't forget to call your energy company to change over ownership! More than one buyer has forgotten to do so, and the power gets turned off at closing if the energy company doesn't know to whom the account should be transferred. You should also factor in moving costs and home insurance. Most buyers tell me, if they are

YOUR TOOL KIT FOR HOME SELLING AND BUYING

getting house warming gifts, gift cards from a building supply company are popular. You never know what you'll need after you move in.

CHAPTER 8

Why Should I Hire Dave Cochrane?

I wrote this book, *Your Tool Kit for Home Selling and Buying: The Answers to All the Mysteries*. Do you know another Realtor who has taken the time, patience and expertise to write a book to help you when buying or selling a house? It's all in here.

I'm a full-time twenty-four-year Realtor, and as everyone knows, *there is no substitute for experience.* I've saved thousands of dollars for buyers and sellers over the years by knowing advanced negotiating techniques. I'm licensed to sell real-estate anywhere in New Brunswick, but being a Saint John native and living in the greater Saint John area, I service Grand Bay-Westfield, Saint John, Rothesay, Quispamsis, and Hampton. I'm a residential specialist, and I've sold homes in all areas of Southern New Brunswick. If I have a buyer here who is planning on moving to another New Brunswick market and I take the buyer there to show them houses, I'm not doing the buyer any favours. I don't know that market as well as a local Realtor so I'd refer the buyers to a Realtor in that market.

If for any reason your personal situation changes and you decide not to sell your home, or I don't do what I said I'd do, I'll rip up the listing.

Currently the average sale price through the Saint John Real Estate Board compared to average list price is 95 percent. Mine average more. It takes about 120 days to sell a house in the Saint John area—mine are selling quicker.

When I get a listing, I have a program that sends the listing to over three hundred real-estate-related websites worldwide for extra exposure. I believe I am the only Realtor doing this innovative marketing in this area.

I produce *virtual tours* for my listings. Pictures of the house set to music with explanations on each picture of what the buyer is viewing. It's marketed all over the world.

I produce a monthly one-minute video with me on camera talking about the current local real estate sales market. It's on the front page of my web site for easy access. It's also sent to hundreds of subscribers. I'm in contact with these people to help attract buyers and sellers.

I use direct mail and social media ad campaigns throughout the year, which also helps attract buyers and sellers.

YOUR TOOL KIT FOR HOME SELLING AND BUYING

I'll always call you back after showings. That's a pet peeve with a lot of sellers. The Realtor doesn't get back to them after the showing. You'll hear from me as soon as I find out, through the buyer Realtor, what the buyers thought of the house.

I have my own dedicated website, www.davecochrane.com, where your home is advertised 24-7 on the front page.

I'm a member of my company's Worldwide Hall of Fame for my home selling and buying production levels.

Conclusion

There you have it. I could tell you it's easy to buy or sell a house. It's not, but the truth is that if you have a Realtor helping you it is a lot easier. I hope this book has answered your questions and cast aside many of your worries about the home selling/buying process. Clients of mine frequently tell me they have no idea how the system works. That's OK. That's why I'm here. I take care of everything and make sure you don't fall down a slippery slope along the way. The examples and issues I've mentioned in the book have come from years of experience listening to and working with buyers and sellers. The opinions are mine and mine alone. Feel free to contact me anytime if you're thinking of buying you first home or selling and buying another. If you know someone who may be selling or buying a house, I would appreciate it if you let me know of his or her interest. I will pay you a thank you fee if they buy or sell a house through me. They may also appreciate a FREE copy of this book. Just let me know. I'm here to help.

GLOSSARY OF TERMS

Breaker panel: This panel distributes power to the house through circuit switches as opposed to older fuse panels. They're safer.

Broker: This is the owner of a real-estate franchise, also called an agent.

Canada Mortgage and Housing Corporation (CMHC): It provides, among other things, loan insurance for federally regulated lenders in Canada when a home buyer has less than 20 percent down payment. This insurance protects the mortgage lender against loss if a borrower defaults and allows qualified borrowers to access homeownership at interest rates comparable to those offered to buyers with larger down payments.

Canadian Real Estate Association, CREA: This organization works on behalf of the public and its Realtor members. It represents the interests of its members to the federal government on issues that affect the members and public. It better assists its members by providing quality technology. It provides national standards, ethics for its members, and up-to-date information and analysis on economic issues.

Closing: The time that title transfers to the new owner.

CMA: Comparative Market Analysis focuses on what houses like the seller's home have sold for in the last few years, what houses have not sold and why and which houses on the market would be competition for the seller. From this information, a suggested list price is determined by a Realtor.

Economy: This is effective management of the resources of a community or system. If there is low unemployment, low interest rates, and optimism by the public, it will be a positive economy.

Greater Saint John Market: It is the areas of Grand Bay-Westfield, St. Martins, Saint John, Rothesay, Quispamsis, Hampton.

Home inspector: They work for themselves or are an affiliate of a national company. They typically have had construction or other backgrounds relating to home building. An **inspector** has the training and certifications to perform such inspections. The inspector prepares and delivers to the client a written report of findings after an inspection that typically takes three to four hours.

MLS: In the Multiple Listing System, brokers share information on properties they have listed and invite other brokers to cooperate in their sale in exchange for compensation if they produce the buyer and the buyer buys a property.

New Brunswick Assessment Department: Assessors look at a variety of factors when assessing your property for tax purposes, including the sale prices of homes or properties in your neighbourhood and any recent renovations or improvements that you may have been made to your property.

Realtor: Some people think that all real-estate agents are Realtors. A Realtor is a real-estate professional who is a member of the Canadian Real Estate Association. If you ask a Realtor what sets that individual apart from a regular real-estate agent, it is a higher standard called the Realtor Code of Ethics.

Saint John Real Estate Board: This is an association of over two hundred Realtors that provides services to and sets standards for members. The board preserves and promotes the MLS marketing system to benefit buyer and seller of real property.

www.ingramcontent.com/pod-product-compliance
Lightning Source LLC
Chambersburg PA
CBHW050022230526
45470CB00003B/1087